Loss Given Default of High Loan-to-Value Residential Mortgages

Min Qi and Xiaolong Yang

Office of the Comptroller of the Currency

OCC Economics Working Paper 2007-4

August 2007

Abstract

This paper studies residential mortgage loss given default using a large set of historical loan-level default and recovery data of high loan-to-value mortgages from several private mortgage insurance companies. We show that loss given default can largely be explained by various characteristics associated with the loan, the underlying property, and the default, foreclosure, and settlement process. We find that the current loan-to-value ratio is the single most important determinant. More importantly, mortgage loss severity in distressed housing markets is significantly higher than under normal housing market conditions. Our empirical results have important policy implications for risk-based capital. Key Words: loss given default, residential mortgage, default, recovery, downturn, Basel JEL Codes: G21, G28

The views expressed in this paper are those of the authors and do not necessarily reflect the views of the Office of the Comptroller of the Currency (OCC), or the U.S. Treasury Department. The authors are especially grateful to Ted Durant for sharing his time and expertise, and to Basil Petrou and Mitch Stengel for help in making this study possible. We also thank Mike Carhill, Dennis Glennon, Mark Levonian, Mitch Stengel, Gary Whalen of the OCC, Tsuyoshi Oyama and Masao Yoneyama of Bank of Japan, and the participants in the 2006 Quantitative Risk Forum at the Federal Reserve Bank of Philadelphia and the Basel II Accord Implementation Group Validation Subgroup meeting in May 2007 for comments that have improved this work. Min Qi is the corresponding author: Risk Analysis Division, MS 2-1, Office of the Comptroller of the Currency, 250 E St. SW, Washington, DC 20219, voice: 202-874-4061, fax: 202-874-5394, email: min.qi@occ.treas.org.

Loss Given Default of High Loan-to-Value Residential Mortgages

1. Introduction

Under the new Basel II capital framework,[1] the calculation of minimum regulatory capital under the advanced internal rating-based (A-IRB) approach requires accurate estimation of parameters that determine the credit risk of banks' financial asset portfolios: probability of default (PD), loss given default (LGD), and exposure at default (EAD).[2] While there has been a growing body of research relevant to the modeling and estimation of PD, there are few studies on LGD (or loss severity, which is equal to 1- the recovery rate) to date, but the number has been increasing rapidly.[3]

The growing literature on LGD has covered several areas, including defining and measuring LGD and the correlation between PD and LGD, both theoretically and empirically. The existing literature has also studied various factors that affect LGD. These include: (1) contract characteristics—seniority and security, credit facility type (loan, bond), term or revolving facility, covenant protection, collateral (type, appraisal date, and results); (2) borrower characteristics—profit margin, debt cushion, leverage; (3) differences across industry and industry conditions; and (4) macroeconomic systematic risk factors. Cyclical effects on LGD are also examined, and LGD during economic downturn periods has been compared to LGD under normal economic conditions. Lastly, research has been carried out to investigate the statistical distribution of LGD.

---

[1] International Convergence of Capital Measurement and Capital Standards: A Revised Framework, June 2006, Basel Committee on Banking Supervision.

[2] Effective maturity (M) is also needed for corporate, sovereign, and bank exposures.

[3] Altman et al. (2005a) provide a comprehensive survey of literature on default recovery rates for corporate credit risk. Altman et al. (2005b) contain a collection of papers on recovery risk. Qi (2005) surveys research on LGD in stressed market conditions.

However, the vast majority of these LGD studies are on wholesale exposures, such as corporate bonds and loans. Partly because of the unavailability of public data, very few studies have been done on retail exposures. Clauretie and Herzog (1990) study the effect of state foreclosure laws (judicial procedure, statutory right of redemption, and deficiency judgment) on loan losses for mortgages insured privately (i.e., private mortgage insurance (PMI)) and by government (e.g., Federal Housing Administration (FHA)). They find that judicial procedure and statutory right of redemption extend the foreclosure and liquidation processes and thus are associated with larger loan losses. They also show that deficiency judgment reduces loss severity for PMI that has no incentive conflict due to its coinsurance feature, while deficiency judgment has no significant impact on the recovery rate for FHA insurance, with which incentive conflict arises due to the lack of a coinsurance arrangement. Lekkas et al. (1993) empirically test the frictionless form of the options-based mortgage default theory. They find that higher initial loan-to-value (LTV) ratios, regions with higher default rates (Texas), and younger loans are associated with significantly higher loss severities whereas the difference between contract and current interest rates has no impact on loss severities; consequently, they reject the propositions about loss severity implied by the frictionless form of the options-based mortgage default theory. Crawford and Rosenblatt (1995) extend options-based mortgage default theory to include transaction costs and show theoretically and empirically the effect of frictions on the individual strike price that affects loss severity.

The regression analysis in the above three studies can explain only a small portion of the total variations in loan-level mortgage LGD (R^2 ranges from 0.02 to 0.14).[4] More recently, Pennington-Cross (2003) and Calem and LaCour-Little (2004) study determinants of mortgage

---

[4] The adjusted R^2 of 0.56 to 0.57 reported in Clauretie and Herzog (1990) is from regressions at the state level, not at the loan level.

loss severity based on government-sponsored enterprise (GSE) data, and their regression analysis shows improved explanatory power. The R^2 reported in Calem and LaCour-Little is 0.25, whereas it is 0.95 to 0.96 in Pennington-Cross (2003). Although the latter study reports very high R^2, it uses a much smaller sample and covers a shorter sample period (1995–1999) that contains no serious housing market depreciation.[5] Coupled with the problems in LGD definition and the timing of the current loan-to-value (CLTV) calculation, the findings of Pennington-Cross (2003) should be interpreted with caution.

Overall the existing studies have found that CLTV or LTV are strongly related to recovery rates (Calem and LaCour-Little, 2004; Pennington-Cross, 2003; Lekkas et al., 1993; Clauretie and Herzog, 1990). The age and size of the loan have also been shown to affect mortgage recovery rates (Calem and LaCour-Little, 2004; Pennington-Cross, 2003; Lekkas et al., 1993). In addition, recovery rates are found to vary with state foreclosure laws (Pennington-Cross, 2003; Clauretie and Herzog, 1990), prime or subprime mortgages (Pennington-Cross, 2003), and the relative median income (Calem and LaCour-Little, 2004). These studies are summarized in Appendix 1.

The existing residential mortgage LGD studies, however, have not paid sufficient attention to how LGD would change under housing market downturn conditions, partly because of the lack of reliable mortgage loss data through a complete housing market cycle. The only study we are aware of that quantifies the expected and economic downturn LGD relationship is Calem (2003). However, his results are based on simulated mortgage defaults of a conforming-size residential mortgage portfolio that is hypothetical and geographically diversified. It is not

_____

[5] The sample average LGD in Pennington-Cross (2003) is only 2.1 percent.

3

clear whether the same relationship would still hold if actual loan-level loss experiences were used.

In recent years, retail loans have surpassed wholesale loans in dollar amount and have accounted for the largest proportion in total assets among national banks as well as all commercial banks. Furthermore, residential mortgage is now the largest share of aggregate retail loans of national and all commercial banks. As of June 2006, the total retail and wholesale loans are around $1.87 trillion and $1.32 trillion, respectively, for national banks and are $2.66 trillion and $2.42 trillion, respectively, for all commercial banks. Residential mortgages account for 49 percent of the aggregate retail loans of the national banks and 52 percent of all commercial banks as of June 2006.[6] Given their prominent position in banks' portfolios, retail LGD in general and mortgage LGD in particular have obviously been understudied in the existing literature. The present research intends to fill that gap.

In this paper, we study residential mortgage loss given default using a large set of historical loan-level default and recovery data of high-LTV mortgages from several private mortgage insurance companies. We show that LGD can be largely explained by various characteristics associated with the loan, the underlying property, as well as the default, foreclosure, and settlement process. As expected, CLTV is the single most important determinant. More importantly, mortgage loss severity in distressed housing markets is significantly higher than under normal housing market conditions.

Our study differs from the existing mortgage loss severity studies in several important ways. First, compared to the existing studies on mortgage loss given default, our LGD definition is more comprehensive and closer to the Basel II definition. Besides the unpaid balance and the

---

[6] Source: "Financial Performance of National Banks," *OCC Quarterly Journal* 25(3), September 2006.

recovery amount, we also include the accrued interest, foreclosure expenses (legal and courts), property maintenance expenses, sales costs, and repairs. Most importantly, all cash flows (positive or negative) are properly adjusted and discounted to the time of default. Second, we use a unique data set that has the most observations and covers a long period that contains a complete housing market cycle, at least for the New England and the Pacific regions. It allows us to be the first to explicitly and empirically model economic downturn LGD for residential mortgages. Third, our data also contain the most comprehensive information for each defaulted mortgage, making it possible to include more explanatory variables and to explain loss given default better than most of the existing studies. Finally, most of the existing loan-level studies use conforming GSE mortgages of usual LTV ratios, whereas our sample consists largely of high-LTV, PMI-insured mortgages.

This paper has several important policy implications for risk-based capital. First, although LTV at time of loan origination can be used to segment risk, updated LTV (or CLTV) dramatically improves risk segmentation. Second, the LGD mapping function specified in the U.S. Basel II rules and guidance reflects stress effects that are generally greater than what our sample and analysis suggest but is nevertheless appropriate. Finally, after considering mortgage insurance payment, the 10 percent supervisory LGD floor required in the U.S. and international Basel II rules for residential mortgage exposures is binding when applied to the average LGD in the MICA sample. However, it becomes less binding if applied to downturn LGD.

The rest of the paper is organized as the follows. In section 2, we describe in greater detail the mortgage claim data set that is used in this research. In section 3, we compare average mortgage loss severity across time, geographic regions, and CLTV ranges. Results of regression analysis are reported in section 4. Section 5 addresses the implications of our findings on risk-based capital. Conclusions are provided in section 6.

2. Data and Descriptive Statistics

We use a large and geographically diverse individual loan-level mortgage default and recovery data set from several major private mortgage insurance companies. The data set was compiled by the Mortgage Insurance Companies of America (MICA), the trade association of the private mortgage insurance industry.[7] Traditionally, lenders have required a down payment of at least 20 percent of a home's value. PMI expands homeownership opportunities by enabling home buyers to purchase homes with as little as a 3 percent to 5 percent down payment for qualified borrowers. PMI is basically the private sector alternative to FHA and Veterans Affairs (VA) insurance. Unlike FHA, PMI companies do not insure the total loan balance. The mortgage insurance industry shares the risk of default with the financial institution and the secondary market investor. Sharing the risk provides incentive for all parties to keep the loan payments current. In addition, PMI generally costs less than FHA insurance and is available on a wider variety of mortgage loan products, and it is not subject to maximum loan amounts. Volumes of business for the private and public sectors are cyclical and rise and fall independently of each other. As of 2005, FHA loans made up 19 percent of the total loan dollar volume, VA loans 8 percent, and MICA member loans 73 percent. Of the total number of loan originations, FHA loans made up 23 percent, VA loans 7 percent, and MICA member loans 70 percent.[8]

---

[7] MICA has six members: GE Mortgage Insurance, Mortgage Guaranty Insurance Corporation, PMI Mortgage Insurance Co., Republic Mortgage Insurance Company, Triad Guaranty Insurance Corporation, and United Guaranty Corporation, which represent the majority of the PMI companies in the United States.
[8] http://www.privatemi.com/news/factsheets/2006-2007.pdf

The complete data set consists of 241,293 mortgage insurance claims that were settled between 1990 and 2003. It contains information about the loan, such as the original loan amount, and the type of loan (purchase or refinance, conforming or jumbo). It includes the insurance coverage effective date,[9] and it tells where the property is located (state, zip, census region) as well as what kind of property it is (single family, condo, 2-4 units, etc.). The data set states whether the owner intended to occupy or invest at time of origination, and it includes the original property value and details abut the default (month and year, unpaid principal balance at default, and broker's opinion of property value at default). Further, the data include information about the foreclosure (month and year, whether the property was sold prior to foreclosure, salvage value net of sales costs and repairs[10]) and the settlement date (month and year).

The following descriptive statistics are generated from the entire 241,293 mortgage insurance claims in the data set. The average original loan amount is about $109,000, and the average unpaid balance at default is around $106,000. The average original property value (the lesser of purchase price or appraised value) is $124,000, and the net salvage value accounts for, on average, about 73 percent of the original property value. The broker's opinion of property values at default averages about $100,000.

About 78 percent of the loans in the sample are for purchase and 9 percent for refinance. Most of the loans (91 percent) are conforming. Most of the properties (81 percent) are single-family houses and 97.5 percent are for owner occupancy. Approximately 27 percent of the defaulted properties are located in the Pacific region, 19 percent are in the South Atlantic region, and 13 percent are in the West South Central region. Among the 50 states plus the District of

---

[9] The insurance coverage effective month and year are generally the same as the loan origination month and year.
[10] Salvage value is actual sale price if known; otherwise it is the regression-adjusted broker's opinion of the property value.

Columbia, California has the most mortgage insurance claims, representing 22.5 percent of all claims.

The raw data, compiled by MICA from its member companies, contain many errors and missing values, such as negative loan amount, invalid settlement date, etc. With assistance from MICA experts, the data were cleaned and scrubbed, resulting in 106,891 clean observations that are used for the analysis contained in the rest of this paper. Data exclusion criteria are listed in Appendix 3, and descriptive statistics from the cleaned data are provided in Table 3.

3. Mortgage Loss Severity by Period, Region, and CLTV

The mortgage risk factors of LTV and CLTV are calculated as original loan amount divided by property value at origination and unpaid balance at default divided by property value at default, respectively. We define loss given default (LGD) as[11]

$$LGD = 100 \times \frac{CUPB + ACRINT + FCLEXP + PROEXP - NETREC}{CUPB}, \qquad (1)$$

where $CUPB$ is unpaid balance at default; $ACRINT$ is the interest accrued on CUPB for 3 months at a monthly average of the 30-year fixed conventional commitment rates based on the Freddie Mac weekly survey; $FCLEXP$ is foreclosure expense (legal and courts) and is assumed to be 5 percent of the $CUPB$; property maintenance expenses ($PROEXP$) is assumed to be 3 percent of net recovery ($NETREC$), where $NETREC$ = min($NETSALVAGE$, 1.5*$ORIGVAL$) where $NETSALVAGE$ and $ORIGVAL$ are the salvage value net of sales costs and repairs and original

---

[11] The loss severity defined in Equation (1) is before Mortgage Insurance (MI) claim. The mortgage insurance companies have the option of either paying the maximum percentage of the claim amount or paying the claim in full and taking title to the property. If the MI company exercises the option to pay the claim in full, the loss to the investor after MI is the small difference between total loss and MI claim amount.

property value, respectively.[12] All cash flows are discounted at the 1-year LIBOR from the foreclosure date to the time of default.[13]

We use the repeat-sales house price index (HPI) reported by the Office of Federal Housing Enterprise and Oversight (OFHEO) as a proxy for the housing market conditions. Figure 1 plots HPI in Panel A and the corresponding house price ratio (HPR, defined as the current HPI as a percent of HPI 18 months previous[14]) in Panel B from 1990 to 2003. We consider a housing market is in a downturn if HPR is less than 100. Based on this economic downturn definition and for the sample period from 1990 to 2003, the New England region was in a downturn during the entire period of 1990–1994, and the Pacific region was in a housing market downturn during the latter half of the 1990–1994 period. The Middle Atlantic region was briefly in a downturn from 1990 to 1991 and again from 1994 to 1995. According to the analysis of the claim rate[15] in each calendar year by MICA, the weighted average claim rates are 0.62 percent, 0.58 percent, and 0.51 percent for the periods from 1990–1994, 1995–2000, and 2000–2003, respectively (Table 1). Given the periods of housing market downturns shown in Figure 1 and the high average claim rate from Table 1, the period of 1990–1994 is considered as our economic downturn period.[16]

---

[12] Foreclosure and property expenses are not reported in the MICA data, nor are the accrued interest, the mortgage rate, or the discount rate. These numbers are chosen based on conversations with experts.

[13] LIBOR (London Interbank Offered Rate) is widely used as a reference rate for funding cost. In Basel II context, an appropriate discount rate will reflect the uncertainty of recovery cash flows and the presence of undiversifiable risk, which implies that the appropriate discount rate for IRB purposes likely will differ from the interest rate required under FAS 114 for accounting purposes. Compared to LIBOR, such a discount rate might result in a slight increase in the LGD estimates, but it should not fundamentally alter our major findings and conclusions as the average time between default and settlement in our sample is around 15 months.

[14] An 18-month window was chosen because a short-term drop in housing price might not cause a surge of housing defaults; on the other hand, if the window is too long, one might not observe any drop in HPI.

[15] The claim rate is defined as the number of claims each calendar year divided by the number of contracts in force at the beginning of each calendar year.

[16] Downturn period is defined under Basel II as a period of high probability of default (not high loss given default). In mortgage markets, however, defaults are often driven by drops in house prices, and thus periods of high default rates are often associated with declines in house prices.

Panel A. House Price Index (HPI)

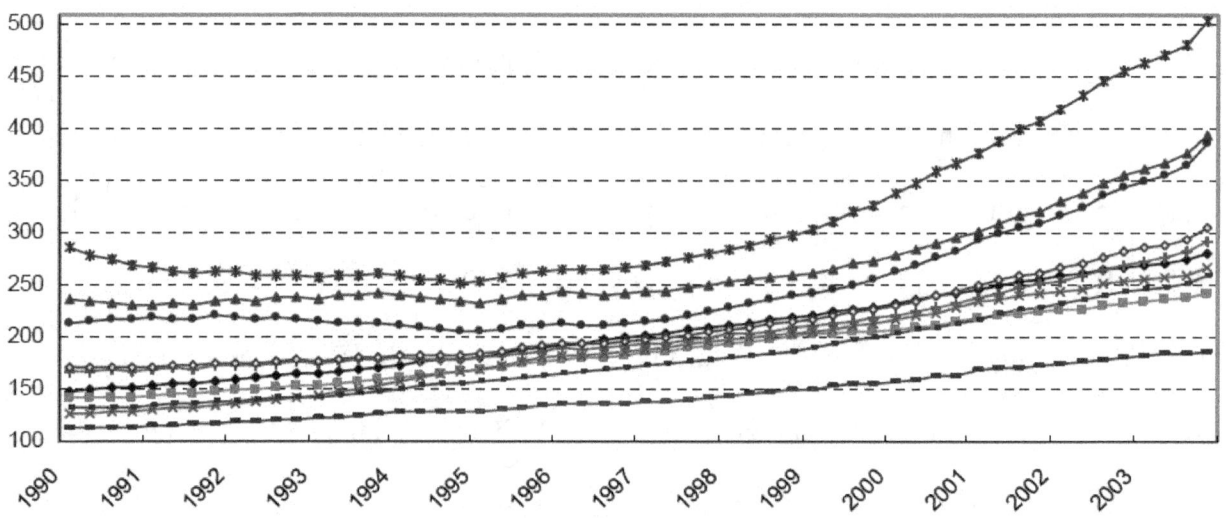

Panel B. House Price Ratio (HPR)=100*HPI/HPI(-18)

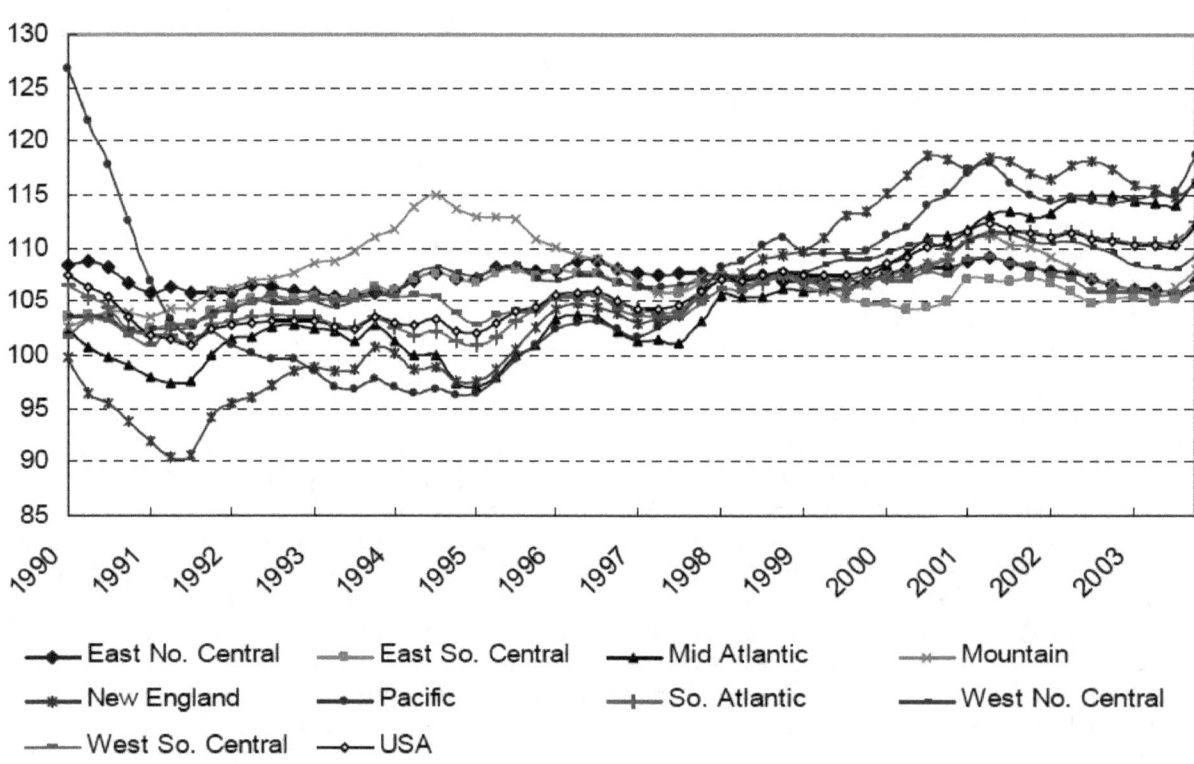

Figure 1. Repeat-sales house price index reported by OFHEO in nine census regions and the United States (1990 to 2003) and 18-month house price ratio

Table 1. Claim Rate

Year	Claim Rate (%)	5-year Weighted Average
1990	0.81	
1991	0.63	
1992	0.60	
1993	0.57	
1994	0.56	0.62 (90-94)
1995	0.49	
1996	0.59	
1997	0.66	
1998	0.64	
1999	0.49	0.58 (95-99)
2000	0.39	
2001	0.37	
2002	0.47	
2003	0.78	0.51 (00-03)

Table 2 provides the summary statistics of loss given default for different CLTV segments, three geographic regions and the United States, during three sub-periods and the entire sample period. It can be observed from Table 2 that loss severity is generally higher during the economic downturn period of 1990 to 1994 in the New England region as compared to other periods and regions. For loans with $80 < CLTV \leq 90$, the mean LGD in New England is 19.3 percent in 1990–1994, which is 5.3 percentage points higher than the mean LGD of 14 percent in the same region during the entire sample period of 1990–2003, and 3.3 percentage points higher than the mean LGD of 16 percent in the whole country during the same 1990-1994 period. This is consistent with the notion that loss severity should vary with the housing market condition in a particular region and during a specific time period. Table 2 also shows the loss severity seems to vary with the CLTV. For the same region and during the same period, higher mean loss severity is often observed with a higher CLTV. This is also consistent with the theoretical and empirical results documented in the existing literature.

Table 2 should be interpreted with caution because the mean loss severity of some of the cells in the table is calculated from a limited number of observations. Table 2 also does not control for other factors that may affect loss severity, such as the loan age and amount, property type, loan purpose, and whether the property was sold prior to foreclosure, etc. In the next section, we study the impact of these and other determinants of mortgage loss severity in a multiple regression framework.

Table 2. Mean Loss Given Default (%) by Year, Region, and CLTV

Default Period	Region	CLTV						
		≤80	≤90	≤95	≤100	≤110	≤120	>120
1990–1994	USA Remainder	4.2	16.3	21.1	24.5	29.9	36.3	48.4
	New England	10.6	19.3	24.2	24.3	30.8	35.5	48.5
	Pacific	3.8	14.0	19.9	23.8	29.0	34.0	43.2
	National	4.5	16.0	21.0	24.3	29.6	35.4	46.6
1995–1999	USA Remainder	4.3	12.2	16.8	19.8	25.0	32.4	45.6
	New England	2.1	11.1	15.8	18.8	24.7	32.2	45.3
	Pacific	-1.0	8.1	13.5	17.7	23.8	30.4	41.4
	National	3.6	11.2	15.9	19.1	24.5	31.4	43.3
2000–2003	USA Remainder	-1.7	9.5	15.3	19.1	24.9	32.2	44.7
	New England	-2.9	5.1	11.4	15.1	22.8	29.5	40.5
	Pacific	-3.8	5.6	12.4	15.5	21.6	28.9	41.6
	National	-2.0	8.9	14.8	18.6	24.4	31.8	44.3
1990–2003	USA Remainder	2.2	12.6	17.6	20.6	26.2	33.4	46.2
	New England	4.9	14.0	17.6	19.8	26.8	33.4	46.6
	Pacific	0.4	9.4	14.9	19.0	25.0	31.3	42.0
	National	2.1	12.0	17.1	20.2	25.8	32.6	44.6

4. Determinants of Loss Given Default

Descriptive statistics of the key variables from the cleaned data are provided in Table 3 (variable definitions are given in Appendix 2). In Table 3, LGD shows considerable amount of variation ranging from -37.3 percent to 84.8 percent, with a mean of 24.6 percent and standard deviation of 16.0 percent. CLTV also varies wildly from 38.8 percent to 170.9 percent with an average of 104.4 percent. The average initial LTV is 90.1 percent, and only 11 percent of the loans have an LTV below 80 percent. These percentages are expected from private mortgage

insurance data.

Table 3. Descriptive Statistics (Variable definitions are in Appendix 2)

Variable	Mean	Std	Min	Max
LGD	24.606	15.962	-37.307	84.820
CLTV	104.429	20.308	38.760	170.900
CLTV080	0.074	0.262	0	1
CLTV090	0.162	0.369	0	1
CLTV095	0.123	0.329	0	1
CLTV100	0.123	0.328	0	1
CLTV110	0.193	0.395	0	1
CLTV120	0.127	0.332	0	1
CLTV120+	0.197	0.398	0	1
HPR	104.345	5.424	78.231	135.573
HPR100	0.205	0.404	0	1
HPR105	0.305	0.460	0	1
HPR110	0.389	0.487	0	1
STRESS	0.204	0.403	0	1
LTV	90.114	5.423	70.863	108.148
LTV080	0.110	0.313	0	1
LTV090	0.450	0.497	0	1
LTV090+	0.440	0.496	0	1
LNSZN	0.916	0.478	0.097	9.938
LNSZN060	0.236	0.425	0	1
LNSZN080	0.254	0.436	0	1
LNSZN110	0.262	0.439	0	1
LNSZN110+	0.248	0.432	0	1
PROPTYPE1SFD	0.852	0.355	0	1
PROPTYPE2CON	0.117	0.321	0	1
PROPTYPE3DUP	0.018	0.133	0	1
LNPURP1P	0.756	0.430	0	1
LNPURP2R	0.235	0.424	0	1
OCCUP1O	0.975	0.155	0	1
PRESALE1Y	0.109	0.311	0	1
PRESALE2N	0.572	0.495	0	1
AGE	58.920	39.320	0	290
AGE24	0.177	0.382	0	1
AGE48	0.322	0.467	0	1
AGE84	0.288	0.453	0	1
JUDICIAL	0.372	0.483	0	1
SRR	0.100	0.300	0	1
NODJ	0.279	0.448	0	1

More than half (51.7 percent) of the defaulted mortgages in our sample have a CLTV greater than 100 percent. This is consistent with the "ruthless" default explanation from the options-based mortgage default theory, which considers default as an optimal decision of rational consumers. Crawford and Rosenblatt (1995) find that when transaction costs are considered, the rational borrower will default only when the value of the collateral falls below the mortgage value by an amount equal to the net transaction costs, such as the costs of moving, brokerage fees, taxes, future deficiency payments, and the stigma associated with default. Since net transaction costs are positive for most borrowers, if the current mortgage balance is close to the market value of the mortgage, the CLTV is expected to be well above 100 percent by the time the rational borrower exercises the default option. Furthermore, Lekkas et al. (1993) show that even if the default option is in the money (i.e., the market value of the house is less than the present value of future mortgage payments), it may not be optimal to exercise the default option because the mortgage claim includes both the options to prepay and also to default at some subsequent date. Reputation costs reduce credit ratings and thus could increase future borrowing costs. This could also be because of the borrower's unrealistic optimism (or wishful thinking) regarding his or her ability to make monthly mortgage payments on time in the future.[17] Finally, our property value at default is obtained by adjusting the broker's opinion of the property value with the house price index (as described in the CLTV definition in Appendix 2). Since the house price indices might overestimate the rate of appreciation on defaulted properties, there may be a downward bias in our estimation of the property value at default, resulting in an upward bias in CLTV.

The CLTV of slightly less than half of the defaulted mortgages in our sample (after scrubbing) is less than or equal to 100 percent, and 23.6 percent and 7.4 percent have a CLTV

---

[17] Wishful thinking and irrational consumer behavior is studied in Yang et al. (2007) and the reference therein.

less than or equal to 90 percent and 80 percent, respectively[18] This may initially look puzzling: Why would anyone default on a mortgage if there were positive equity, i.e., the house value were greater than the current outstanding mortgage balance? In that case, the borrower might be better off selling the property and repaying the debt instead of defaulting. There are several possible explanations. First, selling a house can be a time-consuming and costly process as the transaction cost can easily account for 6 percent or more of the property value. Therefore, selling a home with a 95 percent loan to value ratio could actually result in 1 percent or more loss to the homeowner when a 6 percent transaction cost is factored in. In this case, the person might be better off defaulting and occupying the property "rent free" for a time period from default to foreclosure rather than selling the property and paying back the loan. Second, the broker's opinion of the property value (not the actual sales price) is used to calculate CLTV. It is often the case that the true value of defaulted property is considerably below the fair market value of similar properties in the same neighborhood.[19] An upward bias in the broker's opinion of the defaulted property, which is especially likely if the broker uses a house price index to arrive at his or her valuation, will result in underestimation of CLTV. Third, some of the defaults might be triggered by unexpected non-financial reasons, such as job loss, a significant change in health status, and change in family structure, especially divorce, etc. In these cases the default option is exercised even while it is not "in-the-money" (i.e., these defaults are called "trigger event" defaults as opposed to "ruthless" defaults, see Ambrose et al., 1997 and Pennington-Cross, 2006). Finally, depending on state laws governing mortgage default, the time from default to

---

[18] In comparison, Pennington-Cross (2003) shows that 99.7 percent, 86.2 percent and 38.1 percent of a random sample of Fannie Mae and Freddie Mac foreclosed properties from 1995 to 1999 have CLTV less than or equal to 100 percent, 90 percent, and 80 percent, respectively.

[19] Indeed, the net salvage value averages 73 percent of the original property value in the complete MICA sample, although the worst 18-month house price index depreciation was less than 10 percent in nine census regions from 1990 to 2003.

foreclosure sale can be anywhere from six weeks to eighteen months, during which borrowers enjoy additional benefit (occupying the property "rent free") beyond just the elimination of negative equity but also incur costs (increase the probability of the lender's use of default penalties and deficiency judgment against borrowers' other assets). These costs and benefits must also be weighted at the time of default in determining whether the ultimate put option is in the money (Ambrose et al., 1997).

Also from Table 3, HPR ranges from 78.2 percent to 135.6 percent with a mean of 104.3 percent and a small standard deviation of 5.4 percent. This indicates that on average the house price indices in states where the defaulted properties are located experienced an 18-month appreciation of 4.3 percent with little variation at the state level. The economic downturn indicator has a mean of 0.204, suggesting that 20.4 percent of the defaults happened in states where house prices depreciated in the past 18 months. Only 10.9 percent of the properties were sold prior to foreclosure for sure and for 57.2 percent of the properties were not pre-sold. The average time from loan origination to foreclosure (or settlement if the foreclosure date is missing) is around five years. About 18 percent of defaulted properties in the sample were foreclosed (settled) within two years, and 50 percent within four years.[20]

To get more insight into how the key variables are related, we report in Table 4 the correlation matrix for the following variables: LGD, CLTV, LTV, HPR, loan size, and the number of months from origination to foreclosure (AGE) and from default to foreclosure (FCTIME). There is a very high positive correlation between LGD and CLTV (0.811), a modest negative correlation between LGD and HPR (-0.248), and a modest negative correlation between

---

[20] Loan age is the number of months between the origination date and the foreclosure date (or the settlement date if the foreclosure date is missing). The foreclosure date is missing for around 15 percent of our sample. The average might have been driven up by some outliers, for example, the maximum span from origination to default (or foreclosure) is 290 months in our sample, and the standard deviation is close to 40 months.

CLTV and HPR (-0.183) as expected. Consistent with intuition, Table 4 also shows that initial loan amount is negatively correlated with LGD (-0.056) and with LTV (-0.082), LGD is positively related to the length of the foreclosure process (.099), and larger initial loan amount is associated with earlier default (-.099). There is little correlation (0.002) between CLTV and LTV, and it is statistically insignificant. This may initially look surprising, as one might think, other things being equal, mortgages with higher LTV should have higher CLTV, and thus they should be positively correlated. However, when one analyses the origination mortgage population, it is intuitive and well established that mortgages originated with high LTV are more likely to default. Our sample consists of only *defaulted* mortgages, a subset of all mortgages originated. For this subpopulation CLTV is largely driven by house price movements after origination, thus it may have little correlation with the original LTV.

Table 4. Pearson Correlation Coefficient
(Bold numbers are significant at 0.01% level)

	LGD	CLTV	LTV	HPR	LNSZN	AGE	FCTIME
LGD	1	**0.811**	0.027	**-0.248**	**-0.056**	**0.038**	**0.099**
CLTV		1	0.002	**-0.183**	0.002	**-0.058**	-0.013
LTV			1	**0.061**	**-0.082**	**0.166**	-0.021
HPR				1	**-0.065**	**-0.118**	**-0.104**
LNSZN					1	**-0.099**	0.008
AGE						1	**0.240**
FCTIME							1

4.1. Regression with CLTV

Loss severity can be statistically characterized by conditional means and variances, which are in turn contingent on housing market conditions and on loan and property characteristics. We specify a general regression equation relating loss given default to loan and property characteristics and housing market conditions as

$$LGD_{it} = \alpha + \sum_{j=1}^{J} \beta_j X_{ijt} + \sum_{k=1}^{K} \gamma_k Z_{ik} + \varepsilon_{it} , \tag{2}$$

where LGD_{it} is the loss given default of the ith defaulted mortgage measured at time of default

t, calculated as in Equation (1); X_{ijt} is the value of the jth time-varying explanatory variable for

the ith defaulted mortgage at time t, such as CLTV dummies, economic downturn indicator,

whether the property was sold prior to foreclosure, and loan age indicators; Z_{ik} is the value of

the kth non-time-varying explanatory variable for the ith defaulted mortgage, such as LTV

dummies, loan size dummies, loan purpose, property type, owner occupancy, and state

foreclosure law dummies, etc., that are observed at mortgage origination. The detailed variable

definitions can be found in Appendix 2.

Our sample is very large and there are no obvious violations of the classic regression

assumptions. Thus the model was estimated using ordinary least squares as in Clauretie and

Herzog (1990), Calem and LaCour-Little (2004), and all other studies on mortgage loss severity.

The regression parameter estimates, corresponding p-values, and goodness of fit measures are

shown in Table 5. The model shows relatively high explanatory power ($\overline{R}^2 = 0.662$).

Table 5. LGD Regression with CLTV

Variable	Coefficient	p-value
Intercept	4.239	(.0001)
CLTV090	11.305	(.0001)
CLTV095	17.014	(.0001)
CLTV100	20.527	(.0001)
CLTV110	26.048	(.0001)
CLTV120	32.513	(.0001)
CLTV120+	43.675	(.0001)
STRESS	4.442	(.0001)
LNSZN060	3.540	(.0001)
LNSZN080	1.256	(.0001)
LNSZN110	0.370	(.0001)

PROPTYPE1SFD	-1.344	(.0001)
PROPTYPE2CON	-2.025	(.0001)
LNPURP1P	0.182	(.0082)
OCCUP1O	-1.223	(.0001)
PRESALE1Y	-2.737	(.0001)
PRESALE2N	-0.226	(.0006)
AGE24	-4.046	(.0001)
AGE48	-3.398	(.0001)
AGE84	-2.906	(.0001)
JUDICIAL	0.626	(.0001)
SRR	1.280	(.0001)
NODJ	-3.138	(.0001)
Adj. R-square		**.662**

The impact of the housing market condition is captured in the regression analysis by the explanatory variables of CLTV and economic downturn scenarios. Consistent with the existing studies, loss severity rates are significantly positively related to CLTV (Pennington-Cross, 2003; Calem and LaCour-Little, 2004) and are significantly higher in distressed housing markets (Clauretie and Herzog, 1990). This is also consistent with economic intuition: loans with lower CLTV will have a higher equity value which leads to a higher recovery rate and hence lower loss severity, and vice versa. In principle, if the "true" CLTV could be observed at time of default without noise, and the actual timing and amount of foreclosure and property expenses were available, one might be able to explain close to 100 percent of the variations in LGD. The coefficient of the downturn indicator is positive (4.44) and significant, indicating that, other things being equal, loss severity will be 4.44 percentage points higher in distressed housing markets.

Normalized loan size[21] has a negative impact on loss severity rates. If every other variable is held constant, loans of size less than or equal to 80 percent and 60 percent of median

---

[21] Loan amount is divided by the median home price at loan origination in each metropolitan statistic area or state median price at origination if the former is not available.

home price will have higher loss severity rates, by 1.26 percentage points and 3.54 percentage points, respectively, than those that are greater than 110 percent of median home price. These findings are consistent with observations from the foreclosure process, which contains relatively fixed cost components (for example, attorney fee) at foreclosure and sale of the property regardless of the loan size. These fixed cost components are likely to result in larger LGDs for smaller loans.

Property types of single family and condo have lower loss severity rates, by 1.34 percentage points and 2.03 percentage points, respectively, compared to other property types such as multiple-unit properties. The LGD of owner-occupied properties is 1.22 percentage point lower than the LGD of investment properties. Presale of the property in the process of default to foreclosure will result in a lower LGD by 2.74 percentage points. This finding is consistent with the industry observation in the process of default to foreclosure. Presale will, in general, incur smaller sales and repair costs. The age of the loan has a positive effect on loss severity, consistent with the finding of Calem and LaCour-Little (2004) but inconsistent with those of Lekkas et al. (1993), and Pennington-Cross (2003).

Finally, we find that the LGD is higher in states with a judicial foreclosure process and the statutory rights of redemption. These observations are largely in line with those found in the existing literature. Our results show that the LGD is lower in states where deficiency judgments are prohibited, contrary to what has been found in the existing literature. Based on the framework of Ambrose et al. (1997), in states where deficiency judgment is prohibited, lenders are likely to try hard to shorten the delay between default and foreclosure to reduce the period of the "free rent" and thus the probability of default.[22] This could actually result in lower LGD.

---

[22] According to "Foreclosure Prevention" (Fannie Mae, 1997), the allowable time between referral to the foreclosure attorney and the foreclosure sale date ranges from three to seven months in eight states prohibiting deficiency

Thus our results are consistent with the theoretical framework of Ambrose et al. (1997). Another reason may be that deficiency judgments are rare even when they are permitted because defaulting homeowners are unlikely to have many assets aside from the home and they often protect themselves against deficiency judgments by filing for bankruptcy (Pence, 2006).

4.2. Regression with LTV

The interagency Basel IA Notice of Proposed Rulemaking (NPR) (2006) and Advance Notice of Proposed Rulemaking (ANPR) (2005) on risk-based capital guidelines suggest basing risk weights for residential mortgages on LTV ratios. This will make capital requirements sensitive to risk and will unlikely increase regulatory burden for banks since LTV data are readily available and are often used in the loan approval process and in managing mortgage portfolios. To further assess the relevance of LTV in determining loss severity, we drop the CLTV dummies from the previous regression and add in the LTV dummy variables. The regression parameter estimates and corresponding p-values are shown in Table 6.

Table 6. Alternative LGD Regression with LTV

Variable	Coefficient	p-value
Intercept	30.425	(.0001)
LTV090	2.606	(.0001)
LTV090+	4.527	(.0001)
STRESS	9.442	(.0001)
LNSZN06	2.967	(.0001)
LNSZN08	1.056	(.0001)
LNSZN11	-0.236	(.0753)
PROPTYPE1SFD	-4.368	(.0001)
PROPTYPE2CON	-1.684	(.0001)
LNPURP1P	-3.001	(.0001)

judgments, whereas it ranges from three to 12 months in other states. Indeed, out of the eight states prohibiting deficiency judgments, six do not follow a judicial procedure, and five do not have statutory rights of redemption. It has been documented in the literature that judicial procedure and statutory rights of redemption extend the foreclosure and liquidation processes and are associated with higher LGD.

OCCUP1O	-3.177	(.0001)
PRESALE1Y	-3.591	(.0001)
PRESALE2N	-1.443	(.0001)
AGE24	-0.414	(.0117)
AGE48	-2.075	(.0001)
AGE84	-1.429	(.0001)
JUDICIAL	0.461	(.0001)
SRR	-0.615	(.0001)
NODJ	-0.987	(.0001)
Adj. R-square		**0.070**

In the event of default and foreclosure, the homeowner equity is a function of the initial LTV and the subsequent course of house prices, which vary by geographic region and time period. In particular, the loss severity will increase as the defaulted loan experiences a subsequent house price decline for the 12 to 18 months starting from delinquency. The theory is clearly demonstrated in the empirical estimates from Table 6 as loss severity increases by about 9.44 percentage points in the distressed housing markets where HPI shows decline from its level 18 months ago. The regression results also show that higher LTV at origination leads to higher loss severity at default. The impact of other explanatory variables largely follows the same pattern as observed in Table 5. However, the estimates reported in Table 6 may be biased since the model suffers from omitted variable problem as CLTV, an important explanatory variable, was not included. As a result, the coefficient to STRESS may have a positive bias since CLTV is positively correlated with LGD and STRESS.

Overall the following observations can be made from Tables 5 and 6. First, the following factors—current loan-to-value ratio, stress factor, loan size, property type (single family, condo, etc.), loan purpose (purchase or refinance), whether the owner intended to occupy at origination, whether the property was sold prior to foreclosure, the age of the loan, and the state foreclosure laws—jointly can explain about 66 percent of the variation in the loss severity in the MICA data, which consist largely of high-LTV mortgages (average LTV around 90 percent). Second, CLTV is the single most important determinant of LGD—the higher the CLTV, the higher the LGD. After substituting CLTV dummies with LTV dummies, the adjusted R^2 decreases dramatically from 66 percent to 7 percent. Third, LGD during housing market downturns is statistically significantly higher. The stress factor is especially important in the absence of CLTV; LGD is about 9.44 percentage points higher during economic downturn periods, partly because of the positive bias induced by omitting CLTV in the model. Fourth, CLTV is a much better predictor of LGD than LTV.

5. Implications for Risk-Based Capital Requirements

Our empirical results have important implications for risk-based capital requirements. In the U.S. Basel IA ANPR (2005), the U.S. financial regulatory agencies seek comments on the use of LTV to determine risk weights for residential mortgages and on whether LTV should be updated periodically. Basel IA NPR (2006) proposed more granular LTV buckets for first mortgage risk-weight categories and combined LTV for junior lien mortgages. Our empirical results should shed light on these issues. Furthermore, because of the lack of historical loan-level LGD data, many banks will have difficulty incorporating downturn conditions into LGD estimates at this time and in the near future. A mapping function that transforms expected LGD into economic downturn LGD for regulatory capital purpose has been proposed in the U.S. Basel II NPR (2006) and is required for banks that have not received prior written approval from their primary federal supervisor to use internal downturn LGD estimates. Our results will provide an evaluation of the appropriateness of the proposed adjustment. In addition, there is a 10 percent supervisory LGD floor for residential mortgage exposures except for those guaranteed by a sovereign entity (FHA, VA) in the proposed Basel II rules. The MICA data can also provide information whether the floor is binding for mortgages in various LTV buckets and in different regions. In this section, we discuss these one by one.

5.1. Use LTV to segment risk

Our empirical results in Table 6 show that LTV is statistically and economically significantly related to LGD, and higher LTV is associated with higher LGD. Since regulatory capital is linearly related to LGD, our statistical results thus support the use of LTV to segment risk and the notion that the higher the LTV, the higher the risk weights. However, since our data do not allow for default probability nor expected loss modeling at the appropriate level of granularity, we cannot comment on the appropriateness of the risk weight numbers suggested in Table 3 of the U.S. Basel IA ANPR (2005) and Tables 2 and 3 of the U.S. Basel IA NPR (2006).

5.2. Whether LTV should be updated periodically

CLTV has a much higher correlation with LGD than with LTV (Table 4), and not surprisingly, regression with CLTV has much better explanatory power than that without CLTV (Tables 5 and 6). Furthermore, the average LTV at origination is around 90 percent whereas at time of default, the average CLTV jumps up to 104 percent (Table 3), reflecting a significant decrease in homeowner equity. Therefore, in our opinion, LTV should be updated periodically to better segment risk. However, to calculate CLTV, lenders need to update the property value periodically, which could be quite costly. Alternative approaches could be explored to get a more timely update on property values. For example, the lender could use automated valuation models (AVMs) through vendors or tax assessment, build internal models, or at least adjust the property value using a local house price index. All these alternatives bear some model risk, i.e., the

24

updated property value might differ from the true market value of the property. When the difference is too big, CLTV might become inferior to LTV. Therefore, it is important for banks to follow validation standards on property valuation models (including vendor models) to ensure the model risk is in check.

5.3. Supervisory LGD mapping function

Paragraph 468 of the Basel II Framework requires that loss given default be measured "to reflect economic downturn conditions where necessary to capture the relevant risks." The Basel Committee released in July 2005 new guidance regarding a "principles-based" approach to satisfying the requirements of paragraph 468. In the U.S. Basel II NPR (2006), a supervisory LGD mapping function, $LGD = 0.08 + 0.92 \times ELGD$, has been proposed to transform the long-run default-weighted average LGD to the economic downturn LGD to be used in the regulatory capital requirement formula for banks that are unable to develop acceptable internal downturn LGD estimates. In this section, we examine the accuracy of this mapping function based on the MICA data.

Considering the mean loss severity of the entire sample period (1990–2003) as ELGD, and the mean loss severity of the period 1990–1994 as the downturn LGD, we plot the downturn LGD against ELGD from Table 2 in Figure 2. The dashed line represents the ELGD, and the solid line represents the supervisory LGD mapping function. The dots are the observed downturn LGDs against ELGDs by region (New England, Pacific, and National) and by CLTV buckets taken from Table 2.

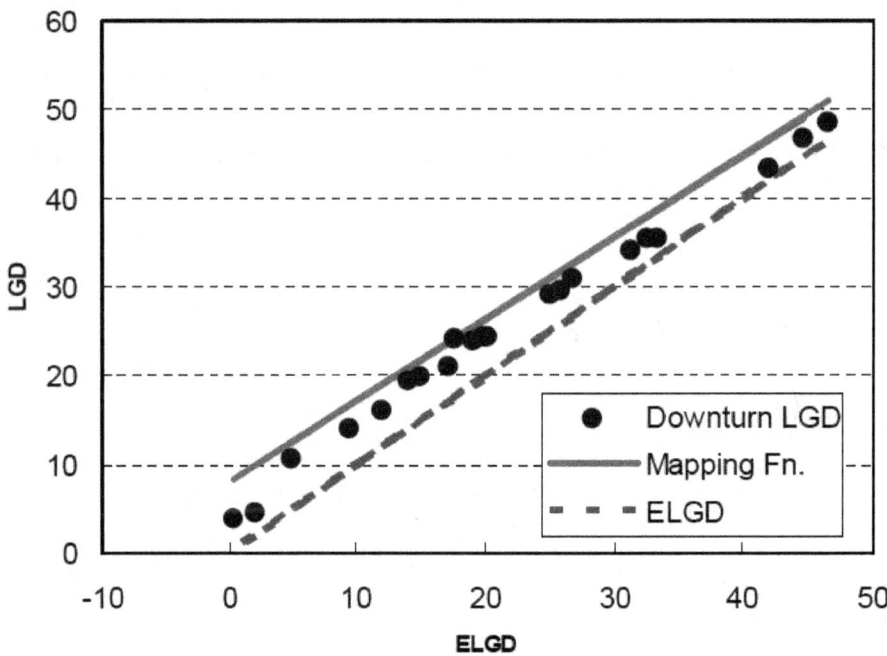

Figure 2. Relevance of the proposed mapping function based on sample LGD

In Figure 2, almost all blue dots lie between the dashed and solid lines, suggesting that in general the supervisory mapping function is somewhat too strict, i.e., it produces higher downturn LGDs than the observed downturn LGDs from the MICA sample. The differences range from -0.008 percent to 5.432 percent, with a mean of 2.497 percent and a median of 2.372 percent.

We further examine the mapping function based on the regression analysis in section 4. Figure 3 plots the downturn LGD against ELGD based on the regression results in Table 5 for seven hypothetical mortgage defaults from seven different CLTV buckets, but with the same and the most typical values for the rest of explanatory variables—the loan size is between 0.8 and 1.1 times the median house price in the area, the loan is for a single-family house, the loan purpose is purchase, the owner intends to live in the property, there is no presale before foreclosure, and the loan age is between two and four years. As discussed in section 4.1, since the CLTV dummies have captured most of the variations in mortgage loss severity, the STRESS indicator has a coefficient of only 4.44. This implies that, other things being equal, the loss severity of a mortgage defaulted during the downturn period will be only 4.44 percentage points higher than a mortgage defaulted during other periods. Consequently, the downturn LGDs are 3.53 (= 4.44 – 4.44*0.204) percentage points above the ELGD (dashed line) and all are below the mapping function (solid line). On average the mapping function gives a downturn LGD that is 2.78 percentage points higher than that from the MICA sample; the median difference is 2.86 percentage points. Thus the supervisory LGD mapping function is somewhat conservative based on the regression model with CLTV dummies.[23]

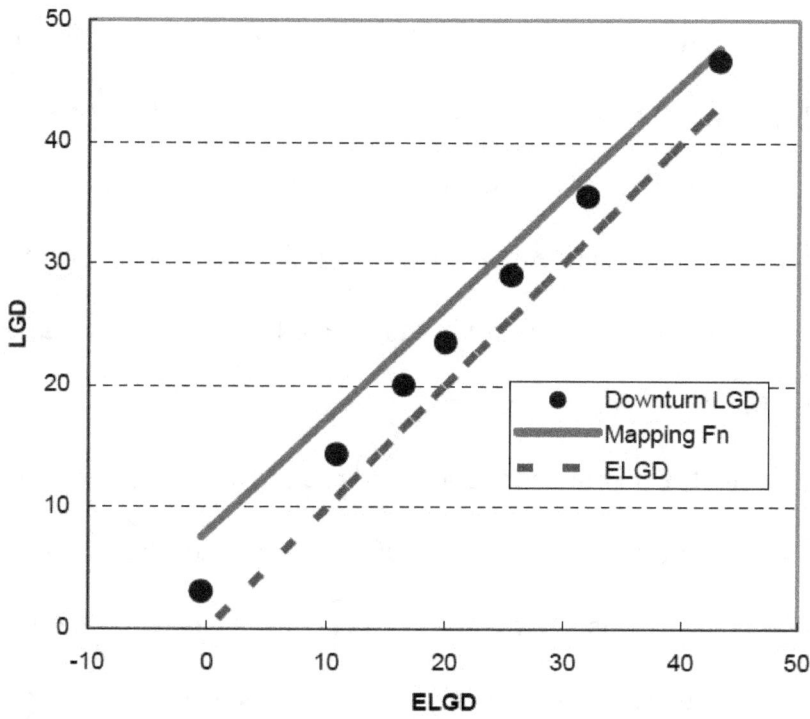

Figure 3. Relevance of the proposed LGD mapping function based on the regression model

---

[23] It should be noted, however, the model in Table 6 suffered from an omitted variable problem; thus, some of the model coefficients (e.g., STRESS) may be severely biased. Consequently, it is inappropriate to draw conclusions about the supervisory mapping function from this model.

5.4. 10 percent supervisory LGD floor

In the U.S. Basel II NPR (2006), there is a 10 percent supervisory LGD floor for residential mortgage exposures, except for those guaranteed by a sovereign entity such as FHA or VA. Before the private mortgage insurance claim benefit is factored in, our sample average LGD is 24.6 percent. Loss severity is less than 7.5 percent for 16 percent of the defaults and is less than 12.5 percent for 27 percent of the 106,891 defaults.

The MICA data does not contain information on mortgage insurance claim benefit, but it can be reasonably well inferred based on common PMI coverage levels and claim handling practices. We assume the coverage level is 12 percent of the claimed losses on mortgages with LTV less than or equal to 85 percent, 25 percent on mortgages with LTV less than or equal to 90 percent, 30 percent on 95 percent, and 35 percent on 100 percent. The mortgage insurance companies have the option of either paying the maximum coverage percentage of the claim amount or paying the claim in full and taking the title to the property. If the mortgage insurance company exercises the option to pay the claim in full, the loss to the lender after factoring in the mortgage insurance benefit is close to zero.

After considering the private mortgage insurance payment calculated as above, the sample average LGD becomes 1.73 percent. Around 78 percent of the 106,891 mortgage defaults in our sample have an LGD that is less than 7.5 percent, and 85 percent of our sample have an LGD less than 12.5 percent. Therefore, the 10 percent LGD supervisory floor is binding for more than 78 percent of the mortgage defaults in the MICA sample. Note, however, these statistics are based on our entire sample of mortgage claims. When applied to the downturn LGD of 9.59 percent (=8%+0.92*1.73%, based on the supervisory mapping function), the 10 percent floor becomes less binding.

6. Conclusions

Using a large set of historical loan-level default and recovery data of high-LTV mortgages from several private mortgage insurance companies, we find that the following factors—the current loan-to-value ratio, loan-to-value at origination, downturn factor (measured by a decline in house price index from a year and a half previously in the state where the property is located), loan size, property type (single family, condo, etc.), loan purpose (purchase or refinance), whether the owner intended to occupy at origination, whether the property was sold prior to foreclosure, the age of the loan, and the state foreclosure laws— jointly can explain most of the variations in the loss severity in our sample (adjusted R^2 of 0.662). We also find that CLTV is the single most important determinant of LGD—the higher the CLTV, the higher the LGD. Substituting CLTV dummies with LTV dummies causes the adjusted R^2 to decrease dramatically from 66 percent to 7 percent. Loss severity in distressed housing markets is found to be statistically significantly higher. In the absence of CLTV, the omitted variable problem causes the stress factor appears to be especially large—LGD is about 9.44 percentage points higher under economic downturn conditions. Finally, LTV is positively related to LGD, but CLTV is a much better predictor of LGD than LTV.

The implications of our study on risk-based capital are the following: LTV at the time of loan origination can be used to segment risk; updated LTV (or CLTV) is the single most important predictor for residential mortgage LGD and thus should be used to segment risk if it is available. Furthermore, the proposed supervisory LGD mapping function appears to be somewhat conservative across geographic regions and current loan-to-value ratios of the

29

exposures, based on both a default-weighted average approach and a regression analysis approach. The conservatism of the supervisory LGD mapping function should give banks incentive to develop their internal downturn LGD estimates and get them approved by their primary supervisors. Finally, the 10 percent supervisory LGD floor is binding for most of the mortgage defaults covered in the MICA sample but may become less binding if only defaults in downturn housing markets were considered.

It is important to note that our empirical results and conclusions are based on defaulted mortgages that are privately insured by MICA members. These mortgages generally have high LTV and represent nearly 10 percent of the U.S. residential mortgage market in terms of both the total outstanding (a little more than 10 trillion as of 2005 year-end) and the total originations (about 3 trillion in 2005).[24] Should PMI mortgage default pattern and loss severity differ from those of other mortgages, such as FHA- or VA- insured, second lien, or mortgages requiring no private mortgage insurance, our findings and conclusions might not apply to other mortgages.

References

Altman, Edward, Andrea Resti, and Andrea Sironi. 2005a. Default Recovery Rates in Credit Risk Modeling: A Review of the Literature and Recent Evidence. *Journal of Finance Literature* 1, 21-45.

Altman, Edward, Andrea Resti, and Andrea Sironi (eds.). 2005b. *Recovery Risk: The Next Challenge in Credit Risk Management*. Riskbooks.

Ambrose, Brent W., Richard J. Buttimer Jr., and Charles A. Capone. 1997. Pricing Mortgage Default and Foreclosure Delay. *Journal of Money, Credit, and Banking* 29(3), 314-325.

Calem, Paul S. 2003. Loss Severity Calculation for Residential Mortgages. Unpublished manuscript. August.

---

[24] Sources: Mortgage Bankers Association and MICA.

Calem, Paul S., and Michael LaCour-Little. 2004. Risk-Based Capital Requirements for Mortgage Loans. *Journal of Banking & Finance* 28, 647-672.

Clauretie, Terrence M., and Thomas Herzog. 1990. The Effect of State Foreclosure Laws on Loan Losses: Evidence from the Mortgage Insurance Industry. *Journal of Money, Credit, and Banking* 22(2), 221-233.

Crawford, Gordon W., and Eric Rosenblatt. 1995. Efficient Mortgage Default Option Exercise: Evidence from Loss Severity. *The Journal of Real Estate Research* 10(5), 543-555.

Lekkas, Vassilis, John M. Quigley, and Robert Van Order. 1993. Loan Loss Severity and Optimal Mortgage Default. *Journal of the American Real Estate and Urban Economics Association* 21(4), 353-371.

Pence, Karen M. 2006. Foreclosing on Opportunities: State Laws and Mortgage Credit, *Review of Economics and Statistics* 88, 177-182.

Pennington-Cross, Anthony. 2003. Subprime and Prime Mortgages: Loss Distributions. Unpublished manuscript. May.

Pennington-Cross, Anthony. 2006. The Duration of Foreclosure in the Subprime Mortgage Market: A Competing Risks Model with Mixing. Working Paper, Federal Reserve Bank of St. Louis.

Qi, Min. 2005. Survey of Research on Downturn LGD. *Basel Accord Implementation Group Work Paper*.

U.S. Basel IA Advanced Notice of Proposed Rulemaking. 2005. Risk-Based Capital Guidelines; Capital Adequacy Guidelines; Capital Maintenance: Domestic Capital Modifications. *Federal Register* 70(202), Thursday, October 20.

U.S. Basel IA Notice of Proposed Rulemaking. 2006. Risk-Based Capital Guidelines; Capital Adequacy Guidelines; Capital Maintenance: Domestic Capital Modifications; Proposed Rules and Notice. *Federal Register* 71 (247), Tuesday, December 26.

U.S. Basel II Notice of Proposed Rulemaking. 2006. Risk-Based Capital Standards: Advanced Capital Adequacy Framework and Market Risk; Proposed Rules and Notices. *Federal Register* 71(185), Thursday, September 25.

Yang, Sha, Livia Markoczy, and Min Qi. 2007. Wishful Thinking in Consumer Credit Card Adoption Decisions. *Journal of Economic Psychology* 28(2), 170-185.

Appendix 1. Summary of Existing Studies on Residential Mortgage Loss Severity

Study	Obs.	Sample Period	Source	LGD Definition	$\overline{R}^2$	Major Findings
Clauretie & Herzog (1990)	408	1980-1987	PMI via Moody's	Direct loss paid/previous year end risk	0.56-0.57	Δr (-), HPA(-), ΔU (+), PS(-), SRR(+), DJ(-)
	85,000	1972-1988 (claims paid)	FHA	(UPB-house value)/original loan amount	0.04-0.05	Δr (-), HPA(-), LTV(+), PS(-), SRR(+)
Lekkas et al. (1993)	9,457	1975-1990 (originated)	Freddie Mac	(UPB-Appraised value)/UPB (UPB-Sale price)/UPB	0.06-0.07*	LTV(+), Age(-), Texas(+), Odds Ratio(+)
Crawford & Rosenblatt (1995)	1,191	1988-1992 (foreclosed)	A large northeastern thrift	(UPB-REO sale price)/UPB	0.02-0.03*	Δr (-), SRR(+), DJ(-)
				(UPB-min(original appraised value, original purchase price))/UPB	0.09-0.14*	Δr (-), PS(-), SRR(+), DJ(-), DIL(-), RTC(+), LPI to foreclosure (+)
Pennington-Cross (2003)	16,272	1995-1999 (foreclosed)	GSEs	(UPB-sale price)/UPB	0.95-0.96	CLTV(+), CLTV*subprime (+), PS(-), DJ(-), Age(-), size(-),size^2 (+)
Calem & LaCour-Little (2004)	120,289	1989-1997 (originated)	GSEs	(UPB-Gross sale proceeds)/UPB	0.25*	CLTV(+), CLTV $\geq$ 90 (-), LTV (-), LTV $\geq$ 80 (-), size (-), size^2 (+), RELINC (-), RELINC^2 (+), Age (+)

Δr: increase in interest rate in the year of termination relative to origination; ΔU: rise in unemployment rate; HPA: house price appreciation; PS: power-of-sale method of foreclosure (non-judicial); SRR: statutory right of redemption; DJ: deficiency judgment; RELINC: relative median income in the property zip code; DIL: deed in lieu indicator; RTC: '1' if the Resolution Trust Corporation disposed the REO property, '0' otherwise; LPI to foreclosure: months from last paid installments to foreclosure: *: indicates R^2.

Appendix 2. Variable Definitions

AGE: loan age, the number of m onths between the origination date and the foreclosure date (or the settlement date if the foreclosure date is m issing). Define *AGE* indicator variables for the following ranges: (, 24]='*AGE24*'; (24, 48]=' *AGE48*'; (48,84]=' *AGE84*'.

BOVVAL: broker's opinion of value, as-is, at default, observed before foreclosure.

CLTV: curr ent loan -to-value r atio or loan -to-value r atio a t tim e of def ault (*t*), defined as
$$CLTV_{it} = 100 * CUPB_{it} / [(HPI_t / HPI_{t_f}) BOVVAL_{it_f}]$$, where t_f is foreclosure date.

Define *CLTV* indicators for the following ranges: (,80]='*CLTV080*'; (80,90]='*CLTV090*'; (90,95]='*CLTV095*'; (95,100]= '*CLTV100*'; (100,110]='*CLTV110*'; (110,120]='*CLTV120*'; (120,)='*CLTV120+*'.

CUPB: unpaid balance at default.

HPI: quarterly house price index, reported by the Office of Federal Housing Enterprise and Oversight (OFHEO).

HPR: house price ratio, defined as $HPR_{it} = 100 * HPI_{it} / HPI_{i(t-18months)}$, HPI_{it} is the house price index of the state where the *i*th pro perty is lo cated at tim e *t*. Define *HPR* indicators for the following ranges: (,100]=' *HPR100*'; (100,105]=' *HPR105*'; (105,110]=' *HPR110*'; (110,)= '*HPR110+*'.

JUDICIAL: '1' ind icates that th e state in which a pr operty is located has a judicial foreclosure process (as opposed to non-judicial or power-of-sale method of foreclosure).

LGD: loss given default, defined as $100 \cdot (CUPB + ACRINT + FCLEXP + PROEXP - NETREC) / CUPB$, where *ACRINT* is ac crued inte rest, *FCLEXP* is foreclosure expenses (legal and courts), *PROEXP* is property m aintenance expenses, *NETREC* is the net recovery. All cash fl ows are discounted at the 1-year L IBOR from the foreclosure date to the time of default.

LNPURP: loan purpose indicator, '1P' for purchase, and '2R' for refinance.

LNSZN: loan amount relative to area median hom e price at origination, i.e., *LOANAMT/MEDPRC*. Define *LNSZN* indicators for the following ranges: (, 0.6]='*LNSZN060*'; (0.6,.8]=' *LNSZN080*'; (.8,1.1]='*LNSZN110*'; (1.1,)='*LNSZN110+*'.

LOANAMT: original loan amount.

LTV: origin al lo an-to-value ratio, d efined as $LTV_i = 100 * LOANAMT_i / ORIGVAL_i$. Define *LTV* indicator variables for the following ranges: (, 80]=' *LTV080*'; (80, 90]=' *LTV090*'; (90,)='*LTV90+*'.

MEDPRC: median home price at loan origination in the metropolitan statistic area, or state median price at origination if the former is not available.

NETSALVAGE: salvage value net of sales cost and repairs. It is the actual sale price if known or regression-adjusted *BOVVAL*.

NODJ: '1' indicates in the state where a property locates deficiency judgments are prohibited.

OCCUP: intended occupancy at origination indicator, '1O' for owner occupies.

ORIGVAL: original property value (lesser of purchase price or appraised value).

PRESALE: property sold prior to forecl osure indicator, '1Y' for yes, and '2N' for no, otherwise unknown.

PROPTYPE: property type indicator, '1SFD' for single family, '2CON' for condo, '3DUP' for 2-4 units.

SALVAGEPCT: net salvage value/original property value.

SRR: '1' in dicates tha t in th e state where a property is located there is statutory right of redemption.

STRESS: economic downturn indicator, '1' if $HPR < 100$ in a state.

Appendix 3. Exclusion Criteria

The following exclusion criteria are applied for data cleaning and exclusion to eliminate potential biases and data errors:

$BOVVAL \leq 5{,}000$

$BOVVAL > 3*ORIGVAL$ or $< 0.5*ORIGVAL$

$CLTV$, LTV, and $SALVAGEPCT$ that are 3 standard deviations away from their respective means

$CUPB \leq 10{,}000$

$CUPB > 1.2*LOANAMT$

$FCTIME < DLQTIME$

$FCTIME \leq 0$

$LGD \leq -50$, or $LGD \geq 100$

$LOANAMT \leq 0$

$NETSALVAGE \leq 0$

$ORIGVAL \leq 10{,}000$

$SALVAGEPCT \leq 0$

$STLTIME \leq 0$